SUPER SANDCASTLE
Animal Habitats

What Lives in the Prairie?

Oona Gaarder-Juntti

Consulting Editor, Diane Craig, M.A./Reading Specialist

ABDO
Publishing Company

Published by ABDO Publishing Company, 8000 West 78th Street, Edina, Minnesota 55439. Copyright © 2009 by Abdo Consulting Group, Inc. International copyrights reserved in all countries. No part of this book may be reproduced in any form without written permission from the publisher. Super SandCastle™ is a trademark and logo of ABDO Publishing Company.

Printed in the United States.

Credits
Editor: Liz Salzmann
Content Developer: Nancy Tuminelly
Cover and Interior Design and Production: Oona Gaarder-Juntti, Mighty Media
Illustration: Oona Gaarder-Juntti
Photo Credits: AbleStock, Eyewire Images, iStockphoto/John Pitcher, ShutterStock

Library of Congress Cataloging-in-Publication Data

Gaarder-Juntti, Oona, 1979-

  What lives in the prairie? / Oona Gaarder-Juntti.

    p. cm. -- (Animal habitats)

  ISBN 978-1-60453-176-3

  1. Prairie animals--Juvenile literature. 2. Prairie ecology--Juvenile literature. I. Title.

  QL115.3.G326 2008

  591.74'4--dc22

                          2008011883

Super SandCastle™ books are created by a team of professional educators, reading specialists, and content developers around five essential components—phonemic awareness, phonics, vocabulary, text comprehension, and fluency—to assist young readers as they develop reading skills and strategies and increase their general knowledge. All books are written, reviewed, and leveled for guided reading, early reading intervention, and Accelerated Reader® programs for use in shared, guided, and independent reading and writing activities to support a balanced approach to literacy instruction.

About SUPER SANDCASTLE™

Bigger Books for Emerging Readers
Grades K–4

Created for library, classroom, and at-home use, Super SandCastle™ books support and engage young readers as they develop and build literacy skills and will increase their general knowledge about the world around them. Super SandCastle™ books are part of SandCastle™, the leading PreK–3 imprint for emerging and beginning readers. Super SandCastle™ features a larger trim size for more reading fun.

Let Us Know
Super SandCastle™ would like to hear your stories about reading this book. What was your favorite page? Was there something hard that you needed help with? Share the ups and downs of learning to read. We want to hear from you! Send us an e-mail.

sandcastle@abdopublishing.com

Contact us for a complete list of SandCastle™, Super SandCastle™, and other nonfiction and fiction titles from ABDO Publishing Company.

www.abdopublishing.com • 8000 West 78th Street Edina, MN 55439 • 800-800-1312 • 952-831-1632 fax

Prairies are wide open fields or meadows. They are covered with grass and flowering plants. Prairies are hot in the summer and cold in the winter.

Canada

NORTH AMERICA

United States
of America

Mexico

☐ = prairies

Where are prairies?

Prairies are in the center of North America.
They extend from Canada almost to Mexico.

What does the prairie look like?

Prairies are mostly flat with a few short hills. Many different animals live together on the prairie.

Grasshopper

Animal class: Insect
Location: North America

Grasshoppers use their long back legs for jumping. A grasshopper can jump 20 times the length of its body! They use their shorter front legs for holding food and walking.

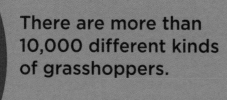

There are more than 10,000 different kinds of grasshoppers.

BULL SNAKE

Animal class: Reptile
Location: North America

Bull snakes are constrictors. They kill their prey by squeezing it to death. Bull snakes eat mice, prairie dogs, gophers, birds, and rabbits.

Bull snakes have a large pointed nose that they use to dig.

RING-NECKED PHEASANT

Animal class: Bird
Location: North America

Ring-necked pheasants are from Asia. In 1857 they were brought to North America for hunting. The male is brightly colored with a white ring around the neck.

The ring-necked pheasant is the state bird of South Dakota.

PRAIRIE DOG

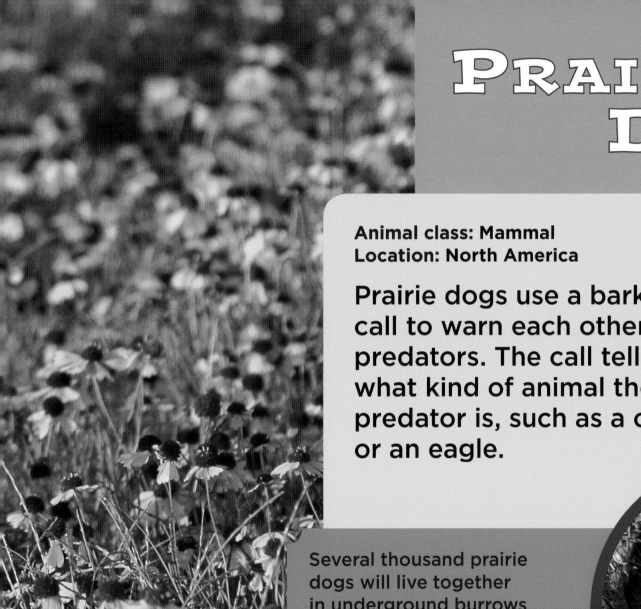

Animal class: Mammal
Location: North America

Prairie dogs use a bark-like call to warn each other of predators. The call tells what kind of animal the predator is, such as a coyote or an eagle.

Several thousand prairie dogs will live together in underground burrows called towns.

NORTH AMERICAN BADGER

Animal class: Mammal
Location: North America

North American badgers have a flat body and short, thick legs. They use their strong legs and sharp claws for digging. They dig shallow dens to sleep in during the day.

Badgers dig prey out of the ground. They eat worms, snakes, frogs, mice, rats, squirrels, and gophers.

PRONGHORN

Animal class: Mammal
Location: North America

Pronghorns are the fastest mammals in North America. They can run faster than 50 miles per hour for short distances. Pronghorns shed their horns once a year.

Pronghorns have large eyes that help them spot predators from three miles away.

COYOTE

Animal class: Mammal
Location: North America

Coyotes are members of the dog family. They live and hunt in small packs. Coyotes communicate over long distances by howling to other pack members.

Coyotes eat mice, rabbits, insects, frogs, birds, lizards, fish, fruits, and grasses.

AMERICAN BISON

Animal class: Mammal
Location: North America

American bison are the largest mammals in North America. Adult males can weigh up to 2,000 pounds. Bison may look big and slow, but they can run up to 30 miles per hour.

Sixty million bison once roamed the prairies. There are 16,000 bison living in the wild today.

Have you ever been to a prairie?

More Prairie Animals

Can you learn about these prairie animals?

black-footed ferret

bumble bee

burrowing owl

fox snake

golden eagle

gopher

jackrabbit

milk snake

monarch butterfly

mourning dove

painted turtle

plains garter snake

prairie chicken

red fox

red-tailed hawk

sandhill crane

skunk

western meadowlark

GLOSSARY

burrow – a hole or tunnel dug in the ground by a small animal for use as shelter.

distance – the amount of space between two places.

horn – a hard, bony growth on the head of an animal.

insect – a small creature with two or four wings, six legs, and a body with three sections.

male – being of the sex that can father offspring. Fathers are male.

mammal – a warm-blooded animal that has hair and whose females produce milk to feed the young.

meadow – an area of grassland in its natural state or used as pasture for grazing animals.

predator – an animal that hunts others.

prey – an animal that is hunted or caught for food.

roam – to walk around without deciding ahead of time where you want to go.

shed – to lose something, such as skin, leaves, or fur, through a natural process.

underground – below the surface of the earth.